田丸稲之右衛門の女 松子

柳水亭種清述

彫栄

女式半棒図解

Women's Hanbo Jutsu

山邊春正

YAMABE HARUMASA

translated by

エリック・シャハン

ERIC SHAHAN

ISBN-13: 978-1721840144
ISBN-10: 1721840141

Tamaru Matsuko 田丸松子 swinging a halberd like a water wheel, from the series *Pictures of Heroic Women* 吾嬬繪姿烈女競 by Tsukioka Yoshitoshi 月岡芳年 1880. Matsuko's father Tamaru Inenoemon got caught up in the Revere the Emperor and expel the barbarians movement at the end of the Edo Era. In a battle in 1865 Matsuko fought and died. Her father was captured and executed in February of the same year.

Translator's introduction

This is a translation of a book on Hanbo, or Half-staff. This typically refers to "half of a Rokushakubo." A Rokushakubo is a staff Six Shaku or 180cm in length. This means the Hanbo is about 60 cm long. The actual length, diameter and tapering of the Hanbo can vary from school to school. The author does not mention any specific length for the Hanbo, but around 60 cm is probably what was used.

This book has pretty clear instruction overall, unfortunately the layout was kind of a mess. The illustrations and the descriptions were often on different pages which required flipping back and forth a lot. It also refers to earlier illustrations which meant even more back and forth.

For this edition the entire book has been reproduced, but the formatting has been improved so that there is a clear division between techniques and the sequence of techniques is shown by reproducing the earlier images.

Some of the transitions between pictures were difficult to understand. I added a few intermediate steps by either reversing the image or "cannibalizing" earlier drawings. These cannibalized drawings, which adapted/altered existing drawings, are labeled with an *.

There are 46 illustrations numbered 1 – 46 however in order to make the techniques easier to follow the numbers have restarted from 1 in for each technique. The numbers above the large illustrations on each page show the original ordering from the book.

Cover of Women's Hanbo Jutsu
1909

Women's Illustrated Guide to Hanbo

Introduction by Hosokawa Masajiro
Former Principle of Chinese Girls School

Introductory Women's History Poem by Shimoda Kako
Head of the Department of Women's Education

Written by Yamabe Harumasa
Shihan of Juken Oga/Yamato School of Martial Arts

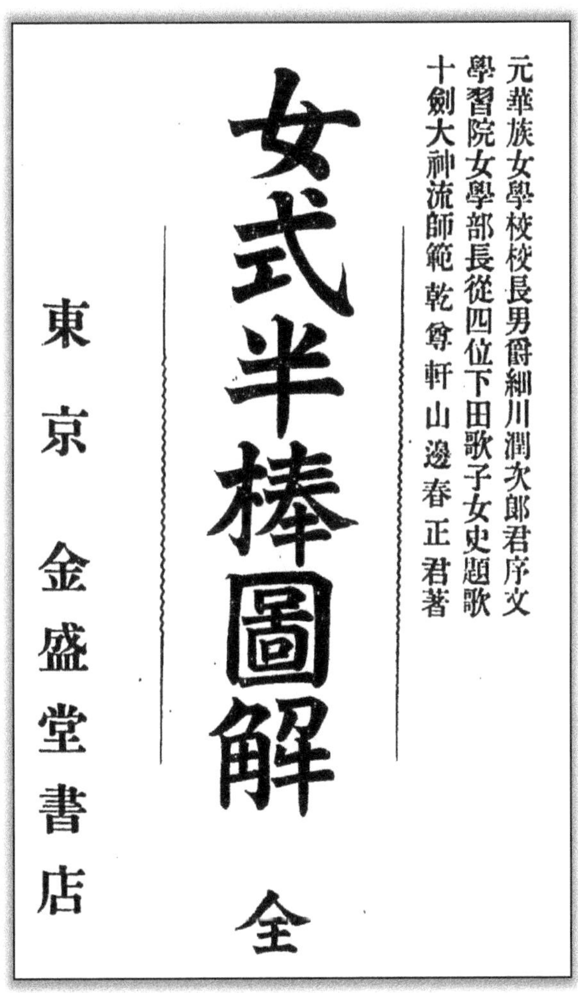

元華族女學校校長男爵細川潤次郎君序文
學習院女學部長從四位下田歌子女史題歌
十劍大神流師範乾尊軒山邊春正君著

女式半棒圖解　全

東京　金盛堂書店

十劍大神流女式半棒圖解

例言

一本書は女子の精神脩養品性維持體育奬勵を目的とし出版せしものなり

一本流は本書を初刊とし柔術薙刀懷劍居合等武術一切の圖解を順次出版せんとす

一本書は初學に便せん爲め韓字に平假名を附したれども再見の字に附せず兒女の記憶を發達せんとするの微意に外ならず

一本書說明に解しかたき場處ある時は本書を携へ來りたるものに限り丁寧に說明を與ふべし

明治三十八年　月　日　編者識

Juken Oga Ryu
The Ten Sword Blessed Japan School
Onnashiki Hanbo Zukai
Women's Illustrated Guide to Half Staff Fighting

Introductory Remarks

One

This book was published with the intent of encouraging and maintaining positive mental and physical health for women.

Two

This is the first book from the Juken Oga School. Future volumes will include Jujutsu, Naginata (halberd), Kaito (knife) Iai (sword drawing.) These will be released as they are finished

Three

In order to make the book accessible to those in the early stages of education all the Kanji have Hiragana beside them the first time they appear. After that students are expected to learn the reading so any succeeding use of the Kanji will not have the Hiragana reading provided.

Four

If there are aspects of the explanation that are unclear we will carefully and thoroughly explain the technique to anyone that brings this book to the Dojo.

38th Year of Meiji 1908
From the Editor

注意

一目附けの事

何づれの場合にても對手の面てを注視するの心得あるべし

一氣合の事

一搆への場合は　ヤー

一打込み又は突の場合は　トー

一受け又は拂ひの場合は　ヤー

Cautions Before Training

One

Where the Eyes Should Look

Throughout training you should always watch the opponent's face.

Two

On the Subject of Kiai (shout unifying the mind and body)

- When you go into Kamae (stance) you should use Yaa!
- When you strike in you should use Toh!
- When you block or sweep an attack away you should use Yaa!

女式半棒圖解の序

棒は一つの武器にして之を用ゐることは一つの武藝なり中にも半棒といへるは稍短きものにて專ら護身の具として用ゐられたり而して其の用法は家家の流義に由りて傳授せしのみにて一定の形式とてはなかりしを此の度山邊春正ぬし古法を斟酌して新に工夫を加へ種々の動作を集めて其の順序を設け繪圖に由りて姿勢を示し簡短なる說明をも附して一つの摺卷とし題して女式半棒圖解と曰へり女流護身の爲にものしたれはなり

抑ゝ女流の武藝に於て薙刀は第一の利器たること疑

Introduction to the Women's Illustrated Guide to Hanbo

The Bo, or staff, is a weapon and there is a corresponding art that teaches its use. Within the topic of Bo there is also Hanbo, or the half-staff. This somewhat shorter weapon is used exclusively for self-defense. However, and this happens frequently, the methods for handling this weapon are held secret by families that transmit the teachings only to the next generation. They never pass the secrets on to anyone outside the family and even if they were keen to do so, each system has a markedly different approach.

Recently, Yamabe Harumasa has, after long reflection, come to the decision to develop and teach a method of Hanbo. To do this she has researched different ways of moving both the body and the Hanbo. The end result was a new system of Hanbo self-defense. Having compiled all this information she titled it *Women's Illustrated Guide to Hanbo*. The purpose of this book is to introduce a method of self-defense geared toward women.

ふへくもあらすされと此は特殊の武器にして常に携帯すへきものにあらす匆卒の際之に代用すへきもののなきに苦むへしさるを此の半棒の如きはいつにても得易きのみならす傘にまれ杖にまれ代用すへきものいくらもありて其の用法にたに習熟するときは應用の道廣くして護身の爲には極めて便利なるへし此れ山邊ぬしか殊更に此の法を世に公にする所以にして余か讀者に告けんと欲する所なり若又此の法を講習するに付けて心膽を錬り身體を健にする利益の如きは一般の武藝に關する所なれは詳にせすともよかるへし

明治三十八年十二月

細川潤次郎

二

There are many that feel that the Naginata, or Halberd, is the martial art best suited to women, however I tend to disagree. The main reason is because it is not a weapon that you have easy access to or can carry about on a daily basis. If you were to suddenly be beset by an enemy you would find yourself at a loss. The lessons learned from studying the Hanbo, however, can be applied to everyday items such as parasols and walking sticks enabling you to defend yourself. If you think about it there are many such items that can be sued in place of a Hanbo.

Having gone through intensive training in this Hanbo method you will be able to apply the knowledge in a wide variety of situations in order to defend yourself. An altogether practical self-defense method. Yamabe, the founder of this school, is now ready to present these techniques to the public. I feel this work is what many readers have been looking for.

If you were to read and train the martial arts techniques within these pages you would be able to strengthen yourself both in body and mind. Clearly this would be very beneficial and reflects the kind of positives found in the more common martial arts. I don't feel I need to elaborate on that anymore.

December of Meiji 39 1909
Hosokawa Masajiro

十劍大神流女式半棒圖解目次

Women's Illustrated Guide to Half Staff Fighting From the Ten Sword Blessed Japan School

Jodan : Fundamental Level Techniques

Shodan : First Stage

Chudan : Intermediate Stage Techniques

上段

通計二十七形四十六圖

Jodan : Upper Level Techniques

Expert Level Techniques

Illustration 1

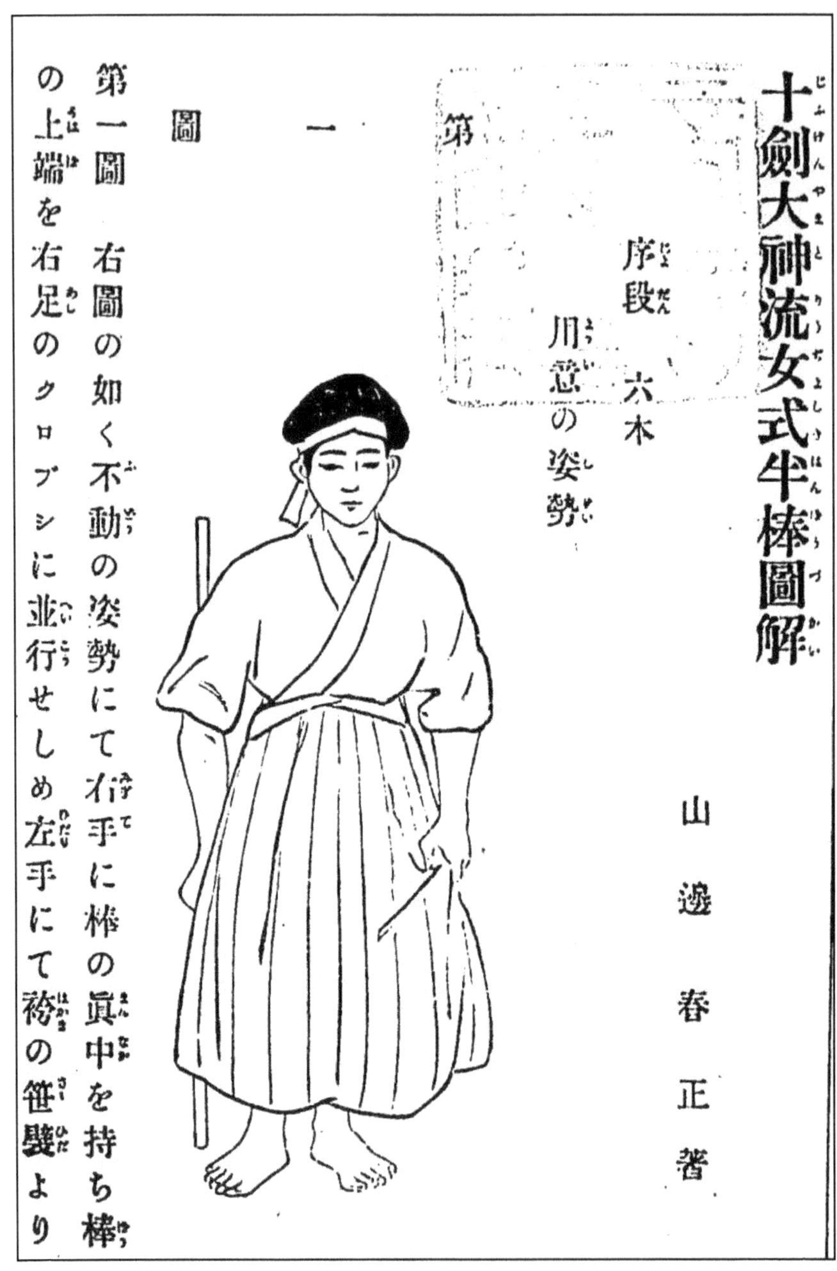

十劍大神流女式半棒圖解

序段 六本

用意の姿勢

山邊春正著

第 一 圖

第一圖 右圖の如く不動の姿勢にて右手に棒の眞中を持ち棒の上端を右足のクロブシに並行せしめ左手にて袴の笹襞より

Juken Yamato Ryu Onnashiki Hanbo Zukai
Women's Illustrated Guide to Half Staff Fighting
From the Ten Sword Blessed Japan School

Yamabe Harumasa

The Jodan, or Fundamental Level, consists of six techniques.

Yoi no Shisei/ Ready Position

Illustration 1 shows the Yoi no Shisei or Ready Position. The feeling of this stance is like the God Fudo, utterly still, but completely ready. The right hand holds the Hanbo in the middle while the lower end lines up with the right anklebone. The left hand grasps the Hakama's Sasahida (seam on the side) and holds it slightly lifted off the ground against the thigh. The Sokusen (toes) should be facing outward.

Illustration 2

By taking hold of both ends of the Staff, you have entered Yoi no Kamae/ The Ready Stance. Following that you should...

股にかけて輕く股立を取り足尖を開くべし

第二圖

第二圖　右圖の如く棒の兩端を持ち用意の構へとなり更に又

二

Illustration 3

...move your hands to the position as seen in the illustration below.

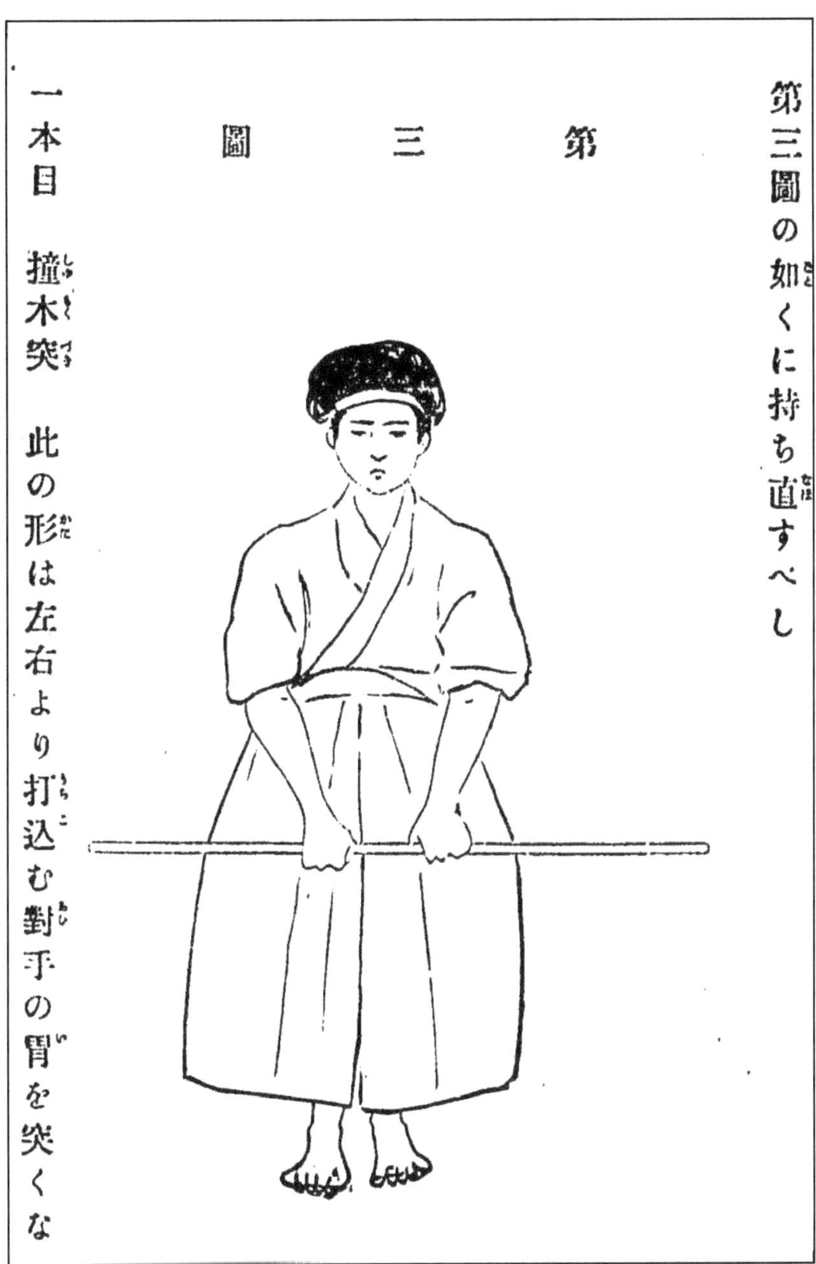

Jodan : Technique 1

撞木突

Shumokuzuki
Piercing Stick Strike

Illustration 4

一本目　撞木突　此の形は左右より打込む對手の胃を突くな

第四圖　右圖の如くに右足其のまま左足を踏出だすと同時に棒を左側に突き出し第三圖の姿勢に復し次に左足其のまゝ右足を踏出すと同時に右側を突き第三圖に復す

Jodan : Technique 1
Shumokuzuki
Piercing Stick Strike.

The intent of this Kata is to respond to an opponent cutting from the left or right by striking them in the stomach.

Start from the stance shown in illustration 1. As illustration 2 shows, step out to the left and simultaneously launch a stabbing strike with the end of your Hanbo to the left. Do not move your right foot. After the strike, return to the stance shown in 3.

Next, keeping your left foot in place, step out with your right foot and, at the same time do a stabbing strike with the Hanbo to the right. Return to the position shown in 3.

Striking to the Left		
1	2	3

Striking to the Right		
1	2	3

Jodan : Technique 2

腰平留

Koshi Hiratome
Side Hip Block

Illustration 5

二本目　腰平留　此の形は對手より脳突横を打ち来るを受け止むるなり

右形は第二圖の構より第三圖の構となり第五圖の如くに棒の下端を左の腰に緊着すると同時に右足を一歩踏み出し之れと共に右の掌を以て棒を前面に押し第三圖に復す左亦之れに倣

Jodan : Technique 2
Koshi Hiratome
Side Hip Block

The intent of this Kata is to block and stop a horizontal strike to your brain (top of the head) by the opponent.

The Kata starts in the stance shown in illustration 1. Next, slide your hands together as shown in illustration 2. Step out with your right foot and pull your left hand down to your hip. Use your right palm to push the staff forward with all your power as shown in 3. Return to the stance shown in 4. Then practice striking to the left.

Striking to the Right			
1	2	3	4

Striking to the Left			
1	2	3	4

Jodan : Technique 3

突棒振打

Tsuki Bo Furui-uchi
Striking Staff Spin and Hit

Illustration 6

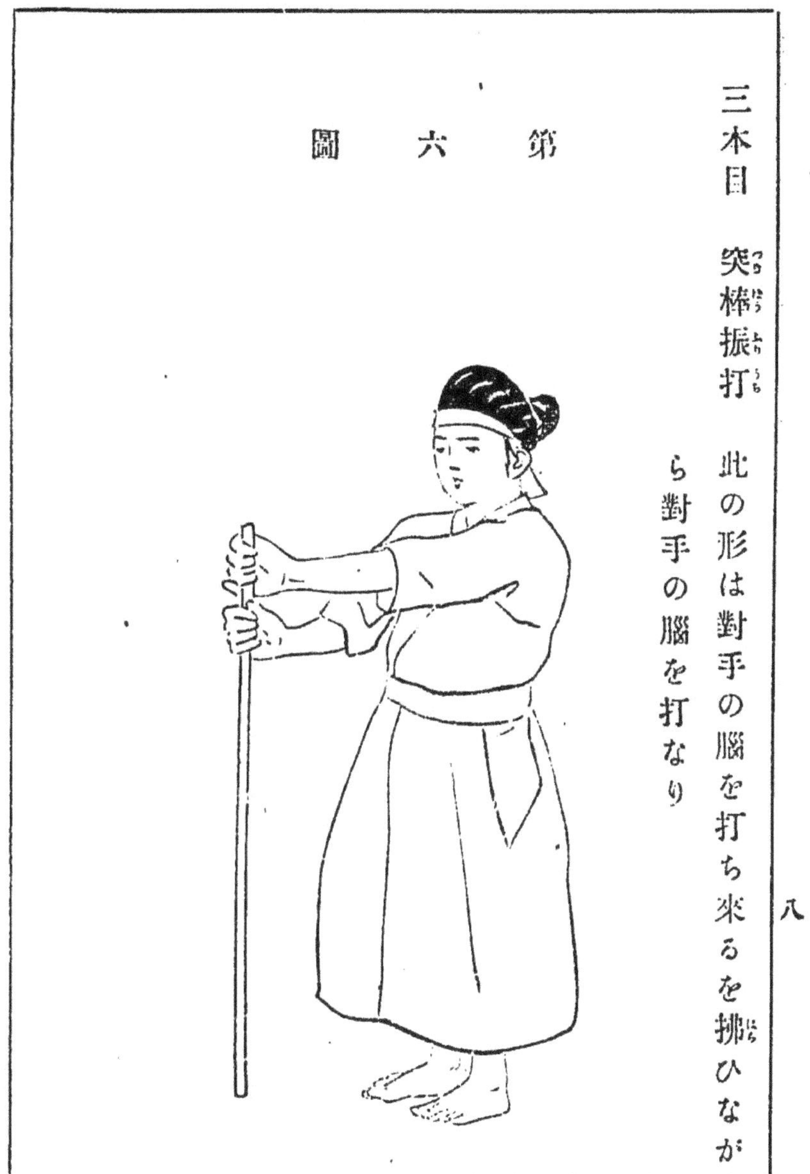

Illustration 7

三本目　突棒振打

此の形は對手の腦を打ち來るを拂ひながら對手の腦を打なり

右の形は第二圖の構へより第六圖の如く棒を前方に突き立て左手其のまゝにし右の足を後方に一歩引くと同時に右の手にて股立を取り左足其まゝ右足を踏み出すと同時に右肩より振り出し第七圖の如くに引きたる足を一歩踏み出し前面を打ち第二圖の構へに復す左も亦之れに倣ふ

Jodan : Technique 3
Tsuki Bo Furui-uchi
Striking Staff Spin and Hit

	In this technique the opponent cuts to your head. The purpose of this technique is to sweep away this attack and then strike the opponent's head. This Kata begins from the stance shown in Illustration 2.
	From there you should do as shown in Illustration 6 by planting the staff in front of you.
	Next, while keeping your left hand in place pull your right foot back one step and allow your right hand to slide down the shaft of the Hanbo. Bring the right hand all the way back to your right hip. * This illustration was not in the original text, it was added to clarify this step. I totally just cannibalized other images to create it.
	Keeping your left foot in place, step forward with your right foot, and release the Hanbo with your left hand. Bring the Hanbo up to your right shoulder and then strike forward. grab the opposite end with your left hand and strike to the side of the opponent's head as shown in Illustration 7. After returning to the stance shown in the second illustration, practice the technique again from the left side.

Jodan : Technique 4

突棒しこき突き

Tsukibo Shigokitsuki
Twisting Stabbing Staff

Illustration 8

Illustration 9

Illustration 10

四本目　突棒しこき突き

此の形は對手の胃を突くなり右は槍法なれば左手充分に張り成るべく體を薄く平らたく構ふるなり

第二圖の構より第八圖の如くに棒を前方に突き立て第九圖の如くに左足を一歩踏み出し右側面し第十圖の如くに二回突き出し第二圖に復す右も亦之れに傚ふ

Jodan : Technique 4
Tsukibo Shigokitsuki
Twisting Stabbing Staff

The intent of this Kata is to stab to the opponent's stomach. Since this is originally a spear fighting technique you should ensure that the left hand grips the shaft firmly and that your chest is slightly.

Starting in the stance shown in illustration 1 transition to 2 with the staff planted on the ground in front of you. Step forward with your left foot while twisting your body flat to the right as shown in 3. Next, as shown in illustrations 4 – 6, launch two consecutive Tsuki, stabbing thrusts. Return to the stance in illustration 7, and practice the technique on the right hand side.

✎ The illustrations below show the sequence with two Tsuki, or stabbing thrusts.

Jodan : Technique 5

つくみ打ち

Sukumi Uchi
Dropping Strike

Illustration 11

Illustration 12

Illustration 13

五本目　すくみ打　此の形は腦を打ち込み來るを體を屈し對手の胃を突き立ちながら對手の腦を打つなり

右の形は第二圖より第八圖の如く右手を上に棒を突き立て第十一圖の如くに體を屈し次に第十二圖の如くに右の足を踏み出し第十三圖の如くに打下ろし右足舊の位置に復すると同時に左の足を踏み出し左の肩より打ち出し其のまま右足を踏み出し第十三圖の如く右肩より打ち出し舊位置に復し第二圖に復す

Jodan : Technique 5
Sukumi Uchi
Dropping Strike

In this technique the opponent is striking to your head. In response you evade by dropping your body and strike to the stomach. Following that, stand and strike to the head.

Begin this technique in the stance shown in illustration 1 and transition to 2 with the staff planted on the ground in front of you.

When the opponent strikes, sink down as shown in 3 and stab to the stomach with the end of the Hanbo. Make sure your right hand is on top. Next, step out with your right foot as shown in 4 and load the Hanbo on your right shoulder. Strike the opponent's head as shown in 5, and then step back with your right foot, returning to your original position but with the staff on your left shoulder 6.

Continuing the attack, immediately step forward with your left foot and strike down from your left shoulder with the staff. Take another step forward with your right foot and strike to the head again. This is shown in illustrations 6 – 9. Finally, return to the stance shown in 10.

- ✐ This sequence consists of one strike to the stomach and three strikes to the head. The first strike is from the right shoulder, the second from the left shoulder, and the third from the right.
- ✐ The illustrations facing the opposite way are to show how the hands should be positioned, they do not indicate striking in the opposite direction.

1
2
3
4
5
6
7
8
9
10

Jodan : Technique 6

刎上げ

Hane Age
Striking Up From Below

Illustration 14

Illustration 15

Illustration 16

Illustration 17

六本目　刎上げ　此の形は對手の打込むを刎上げ棒をしごひて對手の腦を打つなり

右の形は第二圖の棒より第十四圖の如くに棒へ左足を蹈み出すと同時に第十五圖の如くに前方に刎上げ左手其のまゝ第十六圖の如く右手を以て棒を右肩上に引き上ぐると同時に第十七圖の如くに右足を蹈み出し前方を打ち第二圖に復す左亦之れに傚ふ

Jodan : Technique 6
Hane Age
Striking Up From Below

The purpose of this technique is to defend against an opponent cutting to your head. You respond by striking upward from below with the Hanbo. You then allow it to slide through your hand and finally strike the opponent on the head.

This technique starts from the stance shown in illustration 1. Transition to the stance shown in 2, with the end of the Hanbo planted on the ground.

Next, step forward with your left foot and take hold of the Hanbo with your left hand as you do a Hane Age rising strike. You should be positioned as shown in 3. After that, bring the Hanbo up over your left shoulder as shown in 4. As soon as this action finishes step forward with the right foot and strike forward as shown in 5. Following this return to the initial position shown in illustration 6. You should also train this on the left side.

初段七本
Shodan Nana Hon
First Stage
Seven Techniques

Shodan : Technique 1
横突
Yoko Tsuki
Side Strike

Illustration 18

Illustration 19

初段　七本　注意段の變り目の時は第一圖の姿勢より第二圖の構となるべし以下之れに倣ふ

一本目　横突　此の形は對手の胃を突くなり

第一圖の姿勢より第二圖の構となり第十八圖の如くして第十九圖の如く左足を左へ一歩踏み出すと同時に棒を突き出し第二圖に復す左亦之れに倣ふ

Shodan
First Stage

As you are moving on to the next level, it is important that you carefully review the Kamae, or stances, shown in the first two illustrations before beginning the following techniques.

Shodan : Technique 1
Yoko Tsuki
Side Thrust

In this technique you are thrusting into the opponent's stomach. Begin in the Kamae as shown in 1 and then transition into the stance shown in 2. Illustrations 3 – 4 show how you should move the left foot one step outward and, at the same time, strike horizontally with the Hanbo. Return the Hanbo to the starting position. Train striking to the other side as well.

Striking to the Right

Shodan : Technique 2

撞木刎上

Shumoku Haneage
Rising Staff Strike

Illustration 20

Illustration 21

Note: The layout for this illustration was ridiculous. That little bit of Hanbo on the left was on the following page.

二本目　撞木刎上げ　此の形は睾丸又は小手を刎上げ對手の腦を打つなり

右の形は第二圖より第一圖の如く棒の眞中を持ち第二十圖の如く右足一歩前へ踏み出すと同時に刎上げ直に第一圖に復し第二十一圖の如くして背面にて棒を左手に取り直し第一圖の左構をなし刎上げは右に傚ふ

Shodan : Technique 2
Shumoku Haneage
Rising Staff Strike

The purpose of this technique is to first use a rising strike from below to attack the testicles or the wrists of the opponent and then strike them in the head.

This technique starts by holding the bow in the center as shown in 1. Next, switch the bow so you are holding it on your right side like in 2. Attack by taking one step forward with you right foot while sweeping upward with the Hanbo. Use that same hand to bring the Hanbo down on the opponent's head as shown in 3. Bring the Hanbo behind your back and take it with your left hand. Hold the Hanbo in the opposite stance as 1 and repeat on the other side.

- ✎ The wording of this technique is a little choppy. Specifically the transition from the upward strike to the final strike to the head is not entirely clear.
- ✎ The strike to "the testicles or hands" envisions an opponent standing with the sword forward. The strike would be to the groin but if it misses, or the opponent moves, you will hit the bottom of the wrists. The arrow in the illustration below shows roughly the path the Hanbo would take. The picture is of my buddy from France.

1
2
3
4
5

Shodan : Technique 3

横拂留

Yoko Harai Dome
Sweeping Side Stop

Illustration 22

三本目　横拂留

此の形は對手の腦と打ち來たるを横に拂ひ止め對手の横面を打ち小手を拂ふなり

右の形は第二圖より第十八圖の如くし第二十二圖の如く右足を一歩踏み出すと同時に右の手を充分に張り横に拂ひ正面にて棒を留め第二圖に復し第十八圖の左構へとなり左足を踏み出し右の如くに拂ひ第二圖に復す

Shodan : Technique 3
Yoko Harai Dome
Sweeping Side Stop

The purpose of this technique is to sweep aside the opponent's cut to your head and then strike them twice. Once to the side of the head and then a sweeping blow to the wrists.

This technique has three steps. It begins from the stance shown in 1. From there transition to the position shown in 2. Strike as shown in 3 by taking one step forward with your right foot. THe right hand pushes the Hanbo in a sweeping strike to the left side of the opponent's head. Make sure you have put sufficient strength into your right hand. Stop the strike when the Hanbo is directly in front of you. Finally, return to the starting position.

Next, practice the technique on the left side by starting in position 1 and transitioning to position 2. Step forward with the left foot and sweep the Hanbo to the right side of the opponent's head. Finally return to the starting position.

Right Strike		
1	2*	3

Left Strike		
1	2	3

Shodan : Technique 4

平手留

Hira Te Dome
Palm Block

Illustration 23

Shodan : Technique 4
Hira Tedome
Palm Block

The purpose of this technique is to defend against an opponent's sword attack.

This technique begins from the position showed in illustration 1. Transition from 1 to 2 by stepping forward with your right foot and, at the same time, sliding your right hand up the Hanbo. Keep the palm of your right hand flat against the wood, deflect the blow with the center of your staff.

Return to the position shown in Illustration 2.

Shodan : Technique 5

横拂

Yoko Barai
Sweeping Side Strike

Illustration 24

Illustration 25

五本目　横拂　前に同じ　薙刀の法にして五行引き雷形なり

右の形は第二圖より第二十四圖の如く右足を後方に引くと同時に右手の手甲を内に第二十四圖の如くに持ち替へ右足を前方に踏み出すと同時に第二十五圖の如く横に拂ひ右手の手甲を外に持ち換へ次に第二圖に復す右亦之れに倣ふ

Shodan : Technique 5
Yoko Harai
Sweeping Side Strike

This technique begins from the position shown in 1. First, as illustration 2 shows, pull the right foot back and at the same time switch your grip with the right hand from overhand to underhand. Next, step forward and with your right foot and strike to the ribs of the opponent as shown in 4. This strike is called Yokobarai, or sweeping side strike.

At the end of the strike, switch the grip you have with your right hand back to its original position and return to the stance shown in illustration 4.

Shodan : Technique 6 & 7

上段打・上段直打

Jodan Uchi & Jodan Choku Uchi
Upper Strike & Upper Direct Strike

Illustration 26

六本目　上段打（じやうだんうち）　此の形は對手の腕を打つなり
右の形は第二圖より第二十四圖の如く左足を踏み出し棒を持
ち直し第二十六圖の如く上段に取り第七圖の如くに打ち下し
第二圖に復す
七本目　上段直打（ちよくうち）
右の形は第二圖より第二十六圖の如く上段にて打下ろし直（ただ）ち
に右手を引くと同時に上段の棒へに復し二回打ち下し第二圖
に復すべし

Shodan : Technique 6

Jodan Uchi
Upper Strike

The purpose of this technique is to strike the opponent in the head [the text actually says "brain."]

Begin in the stance shown in illustration 1, then step forward with your left foot and raise the Hanbo over your head, switching the grip you have with your right hand from overhand to underhand as you do. This stance, which is shown in 2, is called Jodan, or Upper Stance. Strike as shown in 3 and then return to the starting stance shown in illustration 1.

Shodan : Technique 7
Jodan Choku Uchi
Direct Upper Strike

As with Jodan Uchi, this technique starts from the position shown in illustration 1. You then bring the Hanbo up over your head switching your right hand so you are positioned as shown in illustration 2.

As soon as you are in Jodan, strike to the opponent's head and then pull back with the right hand so you return to Jodan. Immediately strike the head again. After finishing these two strikes return to the stance shown in illustration 1.

中段六本

Chudan Roppon
Intermediate Stage
Six Techniques

Chudan : Technique 1

鳥居巻打

Torii Maki Uchi
Shinto Gate Wrap and Strike

Illustration 27

中段鳥居巻打　此の形は對手の肩を打つなり

一本目

右の形は第一圖より第二圖の構となり第二十四圖の横拂留の構をなし第二十七圖の如くに横上段に取り右足を一歩踏み出すと同時に横斜に打ち下ろし第二圖に復す右亦之れに倣ふ

Chudan : Technique 1
Torii Maki Uchi
Shinto Gate Wrap and Strike

The purpose of this technique is to strike the opponent on the shoulder.

This technique starts from the stance shown in illustration 1 then moves to illustration 2. Slide your right hand down the Hanbo until you are in the stance shown in illustration 3. From that position raise the Hanbo above your head as illustration 4 shows and, stepping out with your right foot, bring the bow down diagonally from above, striking the opponent in the shoulder as shown in 5.

The technique is the same from the other side.

Chudan : Technique 2

横平留

Yoko Hira Dome
Blocking a Side Strike

Illustration 28

二本目　横平留（よこひらどめ）　此の形は對手の胴（どう）と打つを受け止めるなり
右の形は第二圖より第二十八圖の如くに左足を左横に引くと
同時に右向きとなり右擧を以て圖の如く受け留め第二圖に復
す右亦之れに倣ふ

Chudan : Technique 2
Yoko Hira Dome
Blocking a Side Strike

The purpose of this technique is to block a cut to your abdomen.

Begin this technique by standing in the position shown in illustration 1. Next, step to the side with your left foot and, at the same time, twist your body to the left and raise the Hanbo vertically. Your right hand should be flat along the back of the Hanbo. This will block the opponent's attack. Your body should be positioned as shown in illustration 2.

Finally, return to the stance shown in illustration 1.

Chudan : Technique 3

巻れ拂

Makare Harai
Wrap and Sweep Away

Chudan : Technique 4

巻れ進退

Makare Shintai
Wrapping Advance and Retreat

Illustration 29

三本目　巻れ拂　此の形は四方より圍まれし時對手の襟を拂ふなり

右の形は第二圖の構より第二十九圖の如くに左足を引き左向きとなり左を拂ひそれより左足を前へ蹈み出し右向きとなると同時に第二十四圖の構ひとなり第二圖に復す右亦之れに倣ふ

四本目　巻れ進退

右の形は巻れ拂の如くにしつゝ前方へ三步進み次に同樣に三步退く

Chudan : Technique 3
Makare Harai
Wrap and Sweep Away

Use this technique when you are surrounded by the enemy. This technique is a sweeping strike to Eri, the collar.

Begin this technique by standing in the stance shown in illustration 1. Step back with your left foot so your body is open to the left side and do a sweeping strike with the Hanbo in your left hand. This is shown in 2.

Step forward with your left foot again so your body is facing the right and enter the stance shown in 3. Step forward with your right foot and do a sweeping strike with the Hanbo. Finally, return to the starting position shown in illustration 1. Do the technique on the right side in the same manner.

✎ The transition from step two to three is quite vague.

Chudan : Technique 4
Makare Shintai
Wrapping Advance and Retreat

This technique is done the same as Wrap and Sweep Away but you first step forward three steps and end by stepping backward three steps

1
2
3
4*

Chudan : Technique 5

裾拂留

Suso Harai Dome
Blocking a Strike to the Hem

Illustration 30

五本目　裾拂留

此の形は對手より兩足を打ち來たるを受け止むるなり又薙刀槍を受ける法なり

右の形は第二圖より橫拂の構となり第二十七圖の鳥居上段に取り右足を引くと同時に第三十圖の如くに地上を距ること三寸許りの所に打ち下し第二圖に復す右亦之れに傚ふ

Chudan : Technique 5
Suso Harai Dome
Blocking a Strike to the Hem

The purpose of this technique is to defend against an opponent who is cutting with a sweeping strike at both your legs. This technique teaches how to stop this blow and can also be used as a defense against spear or halberd attacks.

This technique begins from illustration 1. Wait in this stance until the opponent begins their cut from the side. When the opponent strikes, simultaneously pull your right foot in and raise the Hanbo above your head. This is shown in illustration 2 and is called making a Torii Shinto Gate shape. Then step forward with your left foot as you swing the Hanbo in an arc downward so that it meets the incoming strike to the Hem of your Hakama approximately 9 cm above the ground. Your body and hands should match what is shown in illustration 3.

Return to the stance shown in illustration 1 and then repeat the technique for the opposite side in the same manner.

Chudan : Technique 6

しごき突き

Shigoki Tsuki
Twisting Stab

Illustration 31

Illustration 32

六本目、しでき突き　此の形は對手の面又は胃を突くなり

右の形は第二圖の構より其のまゝ左足を踏み出し第三十一圖の如く右向きとなり左足を右足に引き付け爪立て直ちに左足を一歩踏み出すと同時に第三十二圖の如き構へにて左足其儘にて二回突き第二圖に復す右亦之れに倣ふ

Chudan : Technique 6
Shigoki Tsuki
Twisting Stab

The purpose of this technique is to stab to the opponent's face or stomach with the Hanbo.

Begin this technique from the stance shown in illustration 1. Step forward with your left foot, keeping your hands in place. Your body will now be facing to the right. Pull your left foot back beside your right foot, keeping just your toes on the ground as shown in illustration 2. As soon as the left foot meets the right, step forward with your left foot and stab forward twice with the Hanbo in quick succession. Your body should be positioned as shown in Illustration 3 after each stab.

Return to illustration one and do the technique on the other side.

Chudan : Technique 7

鳥居上段下構

Torii Jodan Shita Kamae
Upper Torii Gate Lower Stance

Illustration 33

鳥居上段下構

此の形は對手の脳と打ち來たるを體を屈して避け對手を突くか飛び打ちにするか居合法にて地擦り靑眼の構と云ふなり

右の形は第二圖より第二十四圖の前向き一足立の構より取り第三十三圖の如くに兩膝を屈し足尖を地に付け圖の如くに打ち下し構へ立つと同時に第二圖に復す

Chudan : Technique 6
Torii Jodan Shita Kamae
Upper Torii Gate Lower Stance

The purpose of this technique is to avoid the opponent's attack to your head by dropping down and then stabbing the opponent or doing a strike by leaping. This technique is based on Iai, or sword drawing methods. The stance is also known as Jizuri Seigan, or facing the enemy with the end of your weapon scraping the ground.

This technique begins from the stance shown in illustration 1. From there shift to the stance shown in illustration 2, facing the opponent. When the opponent cuts drop down onto your knees with the toes remaining in contact with the ground and your heels off the ground. As you drop down swing the Hanbo up over your head and down onto the opponent. Your body and hands should be positioned as shown in illustration 3. Then return to the stance shown in illustration 1.

✏ Illustration 3 shows the knees together so as you begin your swing you are stepping forward with the right foot to bring it beside the left before you drop down.

上段

Jodan
Advanced Stage
Seven Techniques

Jodan : Technique 1

襟一文字上段構

Eri Ichimonji Jodan Kamae
One Stroke Collar Upper Stance

Illustration 34

上段　襟一文字上段構　此の形は對手の脳を打つなり

一本目

右の形は第一圖より第二圖の構へとなり第三十四圖の如くに右足を踏み出し左側面となり棒を圖の如く襟に掛け左足を出すと同時に左手にて横に拂ひ第二圖に復す

Jodan : Technique 1
Eri Ichimonji Jodan Kamae
One Stroke Collar Upper Stance

✎ The word Jodan (Advanced Stage Techniques) is written the same in English as the previous Jodan (Fundamental Techniques) but the Kanji and meanings are different.

The purpose of this technique is to strike the opponent's head.

This technique begins from illustration 1. Move to hold the Hanbo in front of you as shown in illustration 2. Next, step forward with your right foot, causing your body to face to the left. Bring the Hanbo up onto your shoulders, along your collar, as shown in illustration 3. You attack by stepping forward with your right foot and swinging the Hanbo in a horizontal sweeping strike with your left hand. Finally, return to the position shown in illustration 1.

Jodan : Technique 2

裾拂

Suso Barai
Sweep to the Hem

Illustration 35

Illustration 36

二本目　裾掃　此の形は足を掃ふなり一名犬追物（いぬおふもの）と云ふ

右の形は第二圖の構より左向き襟一文字構と成り第三十五圖の如くに左の手を以て第三十六圖の如くに裾を掃ふべしかくして左右同じ

Jodan : Technique 2
Suso Barai
Sweep to the Hem

The purpose of this technique is to sweep the leg. It is also known as Inu Omono, in reference to the medieval horse mounted archery contest that consisted of shooting blunted arrows at fleeing dogs around a circular track.

This technique begins from the stance shown in illustration 1. Next, turn your head to the left. This stance, the same as illustration 1 except with the head turned, is called Ichi Monji Kamae. This stance is called Ichi Monji because the weapon is making a straight line like the Kanji for the number one, Ichi 一.

From Ichi Monji Kamae, move the Hanbo onto your shoulders at collar level as shown in illustration 2. Then, with your left hand, swing the Hanbo in a sweeping strike to the hem of the opponent's shirt. Your body should be positioned as shown in illustration 3 after this strike. You can attack to either the left or right from the stance in illustration 2.

Jodan : Technique 3

襟一文字雙手打突き

Eri Ichimonji Soshu Uchi Tsuki

Collar One Line Double-Handed Strike and Stab

Illustration 37

三本目　襟一文字雙手打突き

此の形は打つと見せて突くなり

右の形は第二圖の構へより襟一文字構となり右足を踏み出し第三十四圖の如くに構へ第三十七圖の如くに右手を以て打ち下ろし右手を充分に突き出し第二圖に復す右亦之れに倣ふ

Jodan : Technique 3
Eri Ichimonji Soshu Uchi Tsuki
Collar One Line Double-Handed Strike and Stab

The purpose of this technique is to feint and then stab.

This technique begins from the position shown in illustration 1. Then move into the stance Yoko Ichi Monji Kamae, by turning your head to the left. Step out with your right foot and position yourself as shown in illustration 2 with the Hanbo across your shoulders. Use your right hand to swing the Hanbo down onto the opponent's head. At the last second put power into your right arm and turn the downward swing into a stab.

Finally, return to the starting position, illustration 1. The technique is the same on the other side.

Jodan : Technique 4

腰一文字逆拂ひ順直し

Koshi Ichimonji Gyaku Harai Jun Naoshi
Waist One Line Reverse Sweep and Return

Illustration 38

Illustration 39

四本目　腰一文字逆拂ひ順直し

此の形は對手の打込を拂ひ棒を持ち直し打つなり居合法にては首又は胴を斬るの形なり

右の形は第二圖より棒を腰一文字に構へ其まゝ右足を踏み出し第三十八圖の如く腰一文字左構より左手を以て逆横に拂ひ右側面となり棒を第三十九圖の如くに取り直して第二十九圖の如くに左向きに開きしまゝ棒を腰一文字に取り第二圖に復す左亦之れに倣ふ

Jodan : Technique 4
Koshi Ichimonji Gyaku Harai Jun Naoshi
Waist One Line Reverse Sweep and Return

The purpose of this technique is to sweep away the opponent's incoming strike then reset your Hanbo and strike. In Iai, or sword drawing, you can use this technique to cut either the neck or waist.

This technique starts from illustration 1. Keeping the Hanbo in a straight line at waist level, face to the left, this is Ichi Monji Kamae. Next, step out with your right foot and bring the Hanbo around behind your back. You should be positioned as shown in 2. This position is called Koshi Ichi Monji Hidari Kamae, or Waist Left Straight Line Stance.

Use your left hand to swing the Hanbo from behind your back, striking the opponent on his right side with this sweeping horizontal strike shown in illustration 3. This is a Gyaku-Yoko strike, or reverse (since it is from behind) horizontal strike. After this strike you will be facing right now.

At the end of this strike drop your left foot back and position the Hanbo as shown in illustration 4. Then return to the starting position 1.

The technique is the same on the other side.

1
2
3*
4

Expert Level

眞暗撥上拂

Shin no Ami Hana-age Harai
True Rising Strike and Sweep from the Dark

Illustration 40

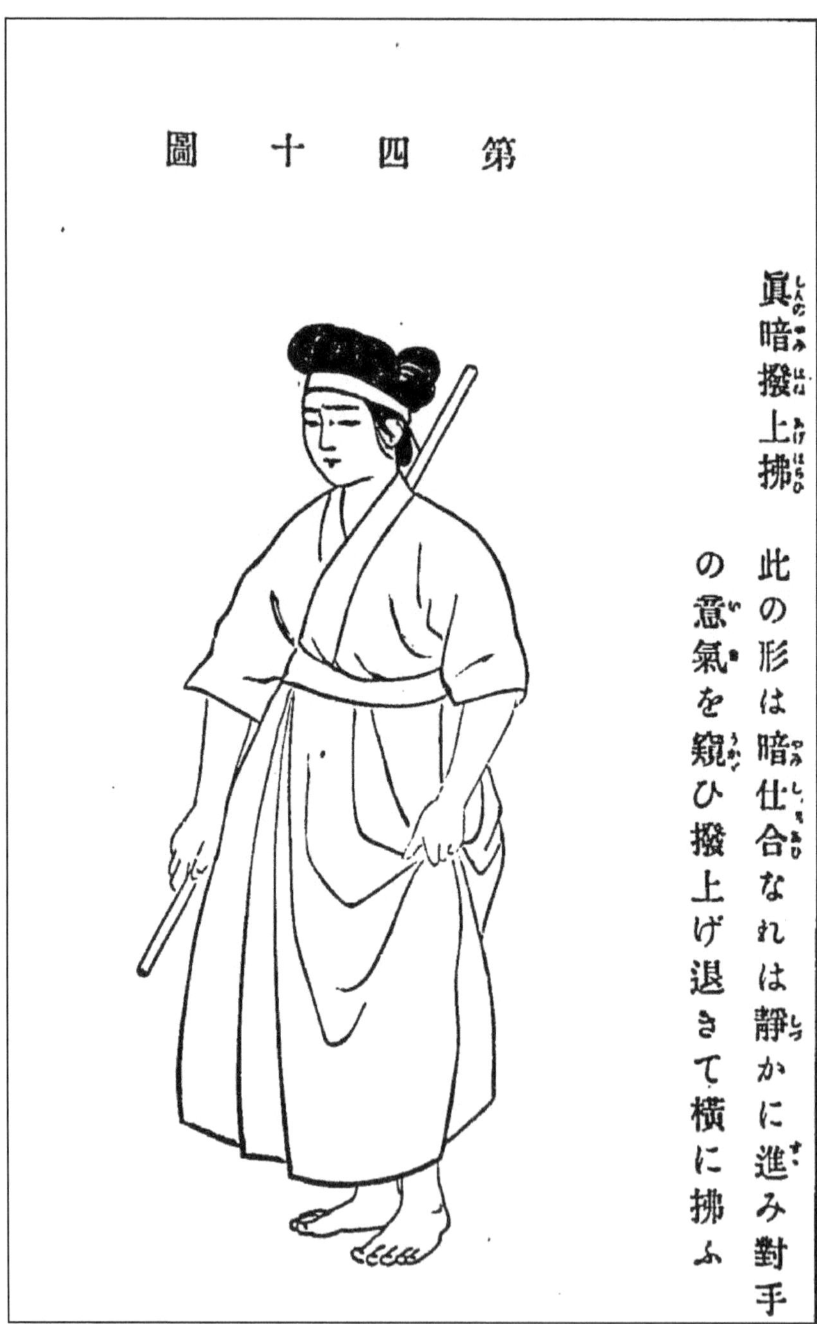

Illustration 41

Illustration 42

Illustration 43

眞暗撥上拂

此の形は暗仕合なれは靜かに進み對手の意氣を窺ひ撥上げ退きて横に拂ふ

右の形は第二圖の構へより第四十圖の如くに左足より四歩靜かに進み第四十一圖の如く棒の下端を以て前面を刎上くると同時に第四十圖に復し爪先にて小足にて舊の位置に復し第三十九圖の如くに棒を取り直し第四十二圖の如くに右足を出すと同時に右手を以て横に拂ひ第四十圖の構となり第四十三圖の如くし右手より背面にて左手に取り直し第四十圖の左構となり第二圖に復す左亦之れに倣ふ

Expert Level
Shin no Ami Hana-age Harai
True Rising Strike and Sweep from the Dark

✐ The following three techniques are in their own category and not associated with the Advanced Stage Techniques. Typically these are called the Okuden or Okugi, "inner mysteries techniques" that require a firm understanding of all the previous techniques. These would not be introduced until the earlier material has been mastered.

This technique is used when you are fighting an opponent in the dark. You are moving forward trying to detect the opponent's presence. When you sense the enemy, attack upward from below, then withdraw one pace and strike with a sweeping horizontal blow.

This technique starts from illustration 1. You then slide the Hanbo up behind your right shoulder, holding the Hanbo near the end. Then, step forward four paces silently, starting from your left foot. This is shown in illustration 2. Next, swing your Hanbo forward and up in a Hane-age, or Rising Strike. Your body should be positioned as shown in illustration 3 with your right foot forward and only the toes of your left foot on the ground.

Then return to the position just before the Hane-age with the Hanbo behind your shoulder, shown in 4. Next, twist your body to the left and allow the Hanbo to slide through your hands so that you are only holding the very end as in illustration 5. From that stance, step out with your right foot and, at the same time, use your right hand to attack with a sweeping horizontal strike as shown in illustration 6.

Next, as is shown in illustration 7, slide the bow across your back from your right hand to your left finally ending in the position shown in illustration 8, but with the Hanbo on your left side. Return to the stance shown in illustration 1 and do the technique on the opposite side in the same manner.

1	2	3
4	5	6
7	8	9

Expert Level

擔構十方打

Ninau Kamae Jupo Uchi
Ten Way Strike From Shoulder Stance

Illustration 44

第四十四圖

擔棒十方打

此の形は一の棒は對手の横面二の棒は胴三の棒は足を拂ふなり

六十九

Illustration 45

第四十五圖

擔棒十方打（にない）

此の形は一の棒は對手の横面二の棒は胴三の棒は足を拂ふなり

右の形は第二圖の棒より第四十四圖の如くに棒を右肩に擔ひ棒へ右の足を出すと同時に右肩より横に拂ひながら右肩にかけ第四十五圖の如くになし左肩より左足を踏み出すと同時に横に拂ひ再ひ第四十四圖の如くにし次に第二圖に復す

Expert Level
Ninai Kamae Jupo Uchi
Ten Way Strike From Shoulder Stance

- ✐ Ninai means "to load onto the shoulder."
- ✐ Juppo means "in ten directions."

The purpose of this technique is to strike the opponent three times. The first strike is a horizontal strike to the side of the head. The second is a strike to the waist and the third is a sweeping strike to the leg.

Begin from the stance shown in illustration 1. Bring the Hanbo up to rest on your right shoulder as shown in illustration 2. Step out with your right foot and swing the Hanbo in a horizontal sweep off your right shoulder to the opponent's head as shown in 3. Push your right shoulder forward to help accelerate the Hanbo. End with the Hanbo on your opposite shoulder as shown in illustration 4.

Step out with your left foot and, at the same time, swing the Hanbo in a horizontal sweep to the opponent's waist as shown in illustration 5. At the end of that attack should be in the position shown in illustration 6. Strike again from your right shoulder but to the opponent's left leg as shown in illustration 7.

End by returning to the starting position, illustration 8.

1 	2 
3* 	4 
5* 	6 
7 	8 

Expert Level
不動上段打
Fudo Jodan Uchi
Immovable (Fully Committed) Strike from Above

Illustration 46

不動上段打　此の形は腦を打つなり居合法にては首を
斬るの形なり
第二圖より第四十六圖の如くに上段に取り右足を一歩踏出す
と同時に前方へ打下し第二圖に復す
但し上段の構は爪先を以て直立すべし

Expert Level
Fudo Jodan Uchi
Immovable (Fully Committed) Strike from Above

The purpose of this strike is to strike the opponent in the head. In Iai, sword drawing, this method would be used to cut the head off an opponent.

This technique begins from illustration 1. From that position bring the Hanbo above your head in a stance called Jodan, as shown in illustration 2. Step forward with your right foot and cut down with the Hanbo at the same time. Finally, return to the position shown in illustration 1.

Note that when going into the Jodan stance you should raise yourself up onto your toes.

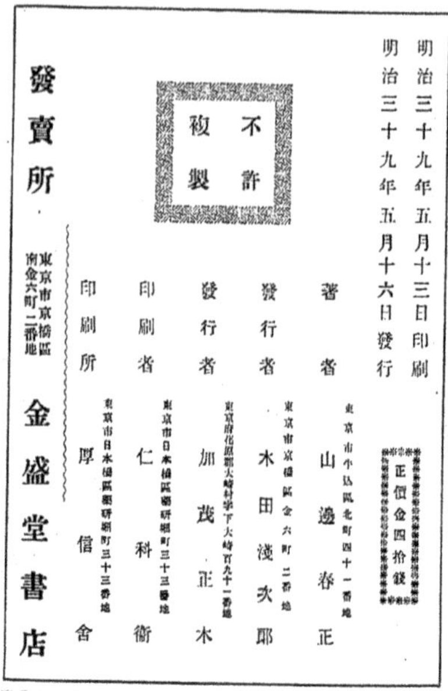

明治三十九年五月十三日印刷
明治三十九年五月十六日發行

正價金四拾錢

不許複製

著者 山邊春正 東京市牛込區北町四十一番地
發行者 水田淺次郎 東京市京橋區金六町二番地
發行者 加茂正木 東京府荏原郡大崎村字下大崎百九十一番地
印刷者 仁科衛 東京市日本橋區蠣殻町三十三番地
印刷所 厚信舍 東京市日本橋區蠣殻町三十三番地

發賣所 東京市京橋區南金六町二番地 金盛堂書店

Published May 16th Meiji 39 1906
Price 40 Sen

- Sen = Japanese penny, 1/100th of a Yen. 1 Yen is equivlent to about 3,800 Yen in today, or about 38 US dollars. So this book would be about $15 dollars today.

- Image of a 50 Sen Coin from the 39th year of Meiji. You can buy these today for about 25$. An uncirculated coin can go for 200~600$ depending on where it was minted.

www.ingramcontent.com/pod-product-compliance
Ingram Content Group UK Ltd.
Pitfield, Milton Keynes, MK11 3LW, UK
UKHW020140250726
13967UKWH00002B/776